CREATIVE EDUCATION • CREATIVE PAPERBACKS

PUBLISHED BY CREATIVE EDUCATION AND CREATIVE PAPERBACKS

P.O. Box 227, Mankato, Minnesota 56002
Creative Education and Creative Paperbacks are imprints of The Creative Company
www.thecreativecompany.us

LIBRARY OF CONGRESS CATALOGING-IN-PUBLICATION DATA

Names: Riggs, Kate, author.
Title: Baby lions / Kate Riggs.
Series: Starting out.
Summary: A baby lion narrates the story of its life, describing how physical features, diet, habitat, and familial relationships play a role in its growth and development.

Identifiers: ISBN 978-1-64026-076-4 (hardcover)
ISBN 978-1-62832-664-2 (pbk)
ISBN 978-1-64000-192-3 (eBook)
This title has been submitted for CIP processing under LCCN 2018939099.

CCSS: RI.K.1, 2, 3, 4, 5, 6, 7; RI.1.1, 2, 3, 4, 5, 6, 7; RF.K.1, 3; RF.1.1

COPYRIGHT © 2019 CREATIVE EDUCATION, CREATIVE PAPERBACKS

International copyright reserved in all countries. No part of this book may be reproduced in any form without written permission from the publisher.

DESIGN AND PRODUCTION

by Chelsey Luther and Joe Kahnke
Art direction by Rita Marshall
Printed in the United States of America

PHOTOGRAPHS by Alamy (Jez Bennett, Carole Deschuymere, Ekaterina Kurakina), Getty Images (Jakub Kaliszewski/Moment), iStockphoto (JNevitt), Minden Pictures (Jurgen & Christine Sohns/FLPA), Shutterstock (Bohbeh, cosma, Eric Isselee, Chris Renshaw)

FIRST EDITION HC 9 8 7 6 5 4 3 2 1
FIRST EDITION PBK 9 8 7 6 5 4 3 2 1

baby LIONS

KATE RIGGS

I Am a Cub	6
Litters of Cubs	8
Hide-and-Seek	10
Eating with the Pride	12
Napping and Practicing	16
I Am a Young Lion	18
Speak and Listen	20
Cub Words	22
Reading Corner	23
Index	24

I AM A CUB.

I am a baby lion.

I weighed only three pounds (1.4 kg) at birth.

My mother hides our litter for one to two months.

I have spots on my fur. I play and hide in the tall grasses.

Then it is time to meet our family. Will they like me?

My pride is my family. Lions are the only cats that live in groups.

My mother and the other lionesses hunt. They share meat with the pride. I eat last.

I still drink milk for six months. I will not start hunting until I am one.

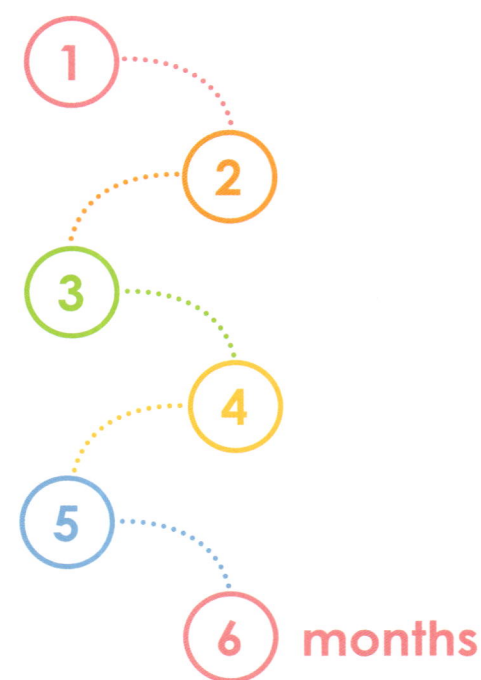

1
2
3
4
5
6 months

We rest in a den when it is too hot. We nap a lot.

My mother starts teaching me how to hunt. I jump and ROAR!

Now that I am older, I can help hunt.

I am a young lion now!

SPEAK AND LISTEN

MEW

WWW!

Can you speak like a cub? Cubs yip and mew. Older lions roar. Listen to these sounds:

https://www.youtube.com/watch?v=pHZm52nvBB4

Now it is your turn!

CUB WORDS

den: a small, hidden area where an animal rests

fur: the hair that covers some animals

litter: the group of animals born at one time

pride: a group of lions that live and feed together

READING CORNER

Bell, Samantha B. *Meet a Baby Lion*. Minneapolis: Lerner, 2016.

Idzikowski, Lisa. *How Lions Grow Up*. New York: Enslow, 2017.

Kelley, K. C. *Baby Lions*. North Mankato, Minn.: Amicus, 2018.

INDEX

dens 16

family 11, 12

food 13, 14

fur 10

hunting . . 13, 14, 17, 18

litters 9

playing 10

prides 12, 13

resting 16

sounds 17, 21

teeth 7

NO LONGER PROPERTY OF
SEATTLE PUBLIC LIBRARY